MW00930052

For You

Records
from Your Lives

Joachim Wolffram

Table of Contents

For You

So you rediscovered me again—me being these notes you left behind for yourself over time. Feel this energy of familiarity, of remembrance. Feel this energy from Home—it was you who compiled me, this text you are looking at.

Feel that this text is more than paper with some printer's ink on it, or more than a screen displaying a few lines, or more than the spoken word reaching you. Whatever the form may be in which you found me again, recognize yourself in me, since you were the one who created me.

During your long journey through your lifetimes, when you had completely forgotten about the purpose of your journey, being in total loneliness, separated from existence, from your love for yourself, suddenly there had been a small point of light. A glimpse of who you really were, a glimpse of your own true nature. It was then that you began to create me. You expressed that glimpse in a little poem. Just a few words, but nevertheless, this poem became your support. You nourished it in your heart, and so, gradually, this little point of light could become a little brighter, spread a little bit more warmth, and become a first step towards ever deepening recognition.

Back then, when your time had come and your death was imminent, you passed this poem on to your son. What else could you have passed on to him? This poem was the most precious thing you had. Over the years, you kept revisiting the magical vibrations of this poem, feeling how recognition can change the past, sensing how this poem was a door to vast secrets about life, and longing to proceed on this path. Back then, you managed to advance as far as you gave yourself permission to. Knowing well that there was so much more and with this great longing to continue on this single true journey, you died—the poem on your lips, your son at your bedside.

Later then, this poem, in a new disguise, under new circumstances, happened to return to you as if by chance. Upon listening to it for the first time, it generated a warm and familiar feeling in your heart. For the first time, you were able to regain your courage, to continue on your path and to let go of your questions about the "why" again and again. You even managed to transcend the poem itself.

Back then, you decided to write the poem down and to express your insights. This was how I was born. Over time, you kept adding more and more to me, providing me with ever new facets. Again and again, you found your way back to me over your lifetimes. Again and again, you recognized me by sensing your resonance with me in your heart. And so, over time, this initially small point of light became like a luminous path to which you were able to find your way back easier and easier.

In fact, the insights contained in me are nothing more than loving helpers created by yourself in order to dive deeper and deeper into yourself, in order to let go more and more of what you see as reality at any given time. These insights are like doors to a deeper understanding. By reading or listening to me in your heart, you are able to walk through these doors easily.

Again and again, you will be afraid of taking a step, another step into an even more profound reality. In such moments, remember. Remember that you were already there at other times. Use me to feel the familiarity of this reality you had already mastered. Feel that you are never alone.

Now, return to the beginning of your story. The beginning of your journey back to you. Back then, when you were totally at a loss about what to do, when all paths had turned out to be blind alleys. Back then, in a brilliant moment of letting go, you all of a sudden experienced .... *silence*. At that time, in that silence, you felt that simply everything in your life thus far—the suffering and despair particularly— had lead to this most important experience of that lifetime. In this intuitive vision, you took the first step back to yourself. This silence inside you only flashed up briefly—it was the point of light—yet it marked the beginning of your journey back to you.

And here, my dear one, your poem from back then returns to you. It still has the same magic, the same capacity to transform time and experience. It is from you for you:

A moment of silence—
And an entire lifetime
Suddenly becomes right.

Your Path

Now that you are approaching yourself again, remember: your path is not an ordinary path. It is not about you wanting to go from here to there and needing to take one step after the other in order to do so. Your path to you will lead via the *letting go* only. Letting go is something you cannot make happen. Letting go is something you can only *allow*, you can only give permission for it to take place. And so your path is rather like dropping—dropping into yourself. This dropping into yourself does not only happen in one particular dimension. In you, there are many, many dimensions. Sometimes, you will find yourself dropping somewhat deeper within one dimension, and at others, you will drop deeper within another one. You will never know in which dimension the next letting go will happen or how deep you will drop, and this will render your journey in every lifetime new and unique in some way.

Over the course of your existence, you accumulated a *huge amount of attachments*. These attachments are so varied that listing them all would simply be impossible. In a nutshell, you can say the following: Whatever you accept as your identity or reality, either *knowingly or unknowingly*, is an attachment.

The ways you are attached to things will determine how you feel about yourself, what your reality looks like and how your environment responds to you. In short: *what you call your life is nothing but your current attachments.*

Begin to see clearly how every attachment creates separation. If you say your nationality is this or that, you automatically separate yourself from all other nationalities. Every attachment will specify you, will draw a line, will split you off—and then you finally say, "This is who I am."

Just look back a few years, maybe ten or twenty. Remember the convictions you had back then— many of which you have probably given up in the meantime. Convictions are a type of attachment. In other words, you *let go* of a few attachments that used to determine you and your reality years ago. No matter how you originally acquired these attachments—it was in your power to let them go. How did you do it? Just like that!

Your attachments have infinitely many layers. They do not originate from your current lifetime only. Many of them you have already been carrying around for a long time, and others are new. Many forms of attachment are obvious, many are hidden—and some are simply taboo. The latter are particularly tricky.

Your path to yourself consists of becoming aware of these attachments and then allowing them to dissolve.

Whatever the attachment may be, you have the power to let it go.

Whenever an attachment dissolves, this will have an immediate impact on your life. As soon as the letting go has happened, not only will you be able to feel the changes inside, but, even more importantly, you will come to notice that your environment will start responding to you differently. Perhaps your letting go will result in you saying farewell to your environment, or those around you will no longer seek to get in touch with you the way they used to because they notice that some kind of bond has been dissolved as a result of your letting go.

In other words, *letting go* generates *change*. *Change*, however, generates *fear*. This fear can be so strong that it might cause you to swerve from your path. This fear comes in many forms: fear of no longer belonging, fear of becoming mad, fear of your own death, fear of claiming too much power, fear of hurting others.

My dear one, in such moments of fear, turn to me and through me remember your long journey. Remember the fact that you will never be exposed to any type of fear that you will not be able to master. Remember how fear gets transformed into joy, and limitation into expansion. Remember most of all that letting go of others does not necessarily imply separating from them. Remember that this process of letting go of human beings and relationships always has something holy—it will make you and others whole, it will guide you and others to wholeness.

Be aware of how paradoxical this is: through your allowing, the letting go can happen. The result of letting go will be change. *There is nothing you have to do.*

One of the reasons you created me was to become aware of the attachments you have not yet noticed in *this* lifetime. Until you are totally free from attachments, until you are the master deciding about your own rebirth, you will tend to constantly recreate attachments, even those you have already shed. You created me in order to help you prevent yourself from continuously turning around in circles, thus enabling you to go deeper and deeper, until you can finally express the unlimited being that you are.

You are wondering what will remain when all attachments have been shed?

Remember the beautiful parable about the onion: What will remain if you peel an onion layer by layer? Everything.

Your journey to yourself is nothing less than the dissolution of your small, limited self back into all that is. Only then, in the harmony of wholeness and individuality, in the unity between spirit and matter, will you revive full beingness.

Remember now that your current lifetime is not just any lifetime. This lifetime is the one you ordained to be *the lifetime*. A lifetime of complete allowing of all letting-go. Remember that this lifetime will be filled with joy, a joy that does not depend on anything and will therefore be totally unlimited and timeless.

Don't Take Yourself Literally

Remember, dear one, that you must not take the words of truth literally. After all, what can one express with words? Who has ever been able to even describe the taste of an apple? Let alone what the vastness of the ocean feels like? For things such as these, words are simply too petty. Therefore do not take me, your words, literally. Do not perceive me with your intellect, but with your heart. Your words are just the carriers of an energy, a particular vibration with which you will be able to resonate again. This vibration has the power to open you once again—if you allow it to happen.

It is as if you were blindfolded, and for the first time after a long while, somebody guided you along the beach of the ocean. Suddenly, a wave splashes some seawater onto your face—now you can taste the ocean, feel its wetness, and these little drops of water enable you to remember the enormous vastness of the ocean. These little drops contain the vibration of the ocean. Your words are like these drops—smell them, taste them, feel them, inhale them, but *do not take them literally*, do not allow your rational mind to chew them, do not even try to *understand* them.

Sometimes you will notice that you are not yet ready to feel the energy of a particular paragraph again. Fine. Return to it at another time. But even if you believe you have absorbed a paragraph completely, *read it again later*, since you have woven a great many layers of meaning into your texts, and some of these levels will only start revealing themselves to you again after another round of letting go of certain attachments.

Back then, when you first let go of words, when you began to understand that no truth can be held on to, let alone be put into words, you wrote a poem. Feel the stillness of your words, feel the freedom behind your words.

Silent Freedom

You. Listen to me! Simply listen.
Listen to what is between the sounds—
This is where Silence dwells.

This Silence
Is the Source.
The Pure Source.

Whatever emerges from it
Is always fresh,
Always new,
Always untainted.

But hold on to something,
And it will die right away,
Even the highest wisdom
Will wither
Immediately.

Look:
Between the sounds,
In the silence,
Is YOU.

Before the word
Is YOU.

What is holding you back?
Which word could have more power
Than YOU yourself?

This YOU is not you —
you—is like a bunker
Made of concrete words.
Congealed.

But look closely:
This bunker isn't any more solid
Than soap-bubbles,
It does not have any more substance
Than a breath of wind.

Now!
Right now!
You, in your bunker made of words,
Listen, listen closely . . .

Listen yourself—
Into freedom.

Religion

Remember, dear one, the many paths of numerous religions you practiced over the course of your lifetimes. Although the path of the ancient ones, the path of tradition, ceremonies, vows and the like was appropriate for particular segments of your path in particular times and in particular surroundings, no religion could and can set you free. Since it is nothing but the attachments you adopted which are veiling your wholeness, ultimately, only you yourself will be able to lift that veil. Love, compassion, truth, profundity and realization cannot be structured. They cannot be managed. They cannot be taught. Remember that nothing alive can ever be *taught*—simply because all life is in a constant state of flux.

Life comes to you in many ways. It is constantly trying to touch you, to get you out of your dreams. Sometimes when something touched you, be it a holy scripture, a ritual, a work of art, a master, you felt so enchanted that you wanted to hold on to it. You wanted to be able to repeat this wonderful experience, this unique moment for yourself, and you also wanted to share it with others, to proclaim it. You had separated from your experience and tried to manifest it in the outside. This way, you contributed to the creation of many religions, you embellished them and tried to spread them. But finally you understood: Every external structure you create or accept is like a prison preventing you from going deeper inside, preventing you from allowing total letting go.

Remember that *every* external help, and therefore also every religion, every form of practice, every technique, is only like medicine. A crutch that will help you continue on your path for a certain period of time. On your way back to yourself, you will gradually need to let go of *any* crutches.

Your personal path to yourself, the experience of letting go ever more profound attachments, is the only religion having the power to transcend itself. It does not have any content, and yet it is sheer abundance. It does not have any external representation, and yet it is obvious. It comes with a particular fragrance, a brightness in your eyes, a gracefulness in your actions, a radiance from the expansion of your heart which will draw the attention of those around you. This, dear one, is something you ought to remember!

Also remember that you cannot help anybody. You can only *be*. Let those around you come if they wish. Let them feel your presence, let them be touched by your warmth and profundity. Reveal the entire potential of everyone through yourself. However, do not allow the responses of those around you to obstruct your journey back to you by holding on to them and by reinforcing them. Avoid supporting others in becoming attached to you. Avoid supporting others in making your path their *ideal*. Avoid embellishing and creating any type of frozen religion. Avoid it for your own sake and out of respect for everybody else.

Dreams

Remember, dear one, the reality of dreams. Dreams are reality. You feel that the dreams you might have at night are very elusive, insubstantial. And so you might be tempted to think that this type of dream is nothing but the result of your consciousness having become weary. Remember that reality is nothing but the agreement of some human beings on how to label and structure sensory perceptions shared by them. For different groups of people, in different cultures or in different ages, the same set of sensory impressions will generate totally different realities. Which of these realities should be the "real" one?

According to your perception, dreams on the physical level will simply unfold more *slowly*, and the objects of the physical dream seem to be more *solid*. But just look inside, look inside a rock, inside a flower—there you will neither find anything solid nor anything slow. In a seemingly magical way, you will find nothing but structured energy there. Energy that is constantly moving.

If something enters your field of perception that nobody else around you is able to perceive, you will gradually begin to suppress this kind of perception. As a result, your reality will become less rich—you will make your dream shallower.

Remember that dreaming together will facilitate manifestation of the dream in the material world.

Joining forces in holding on to the manifestation will therefore preserve what has been manifested.

You are dreaming on all levels of your being, and so you are creating reality on all levels of your being.

Allowing the letting go to happen means being ready to let go of all realities you dreamt into being. The moment you let go of all your dreams in all your dimensions, you will be pure potential, pure being. You will be poised at the point right before creation. Remember that you can return to this point anytime. Remember that creation takes place in every moment.

Remember that you have been endowed with the freedom to dream whatever reality into being and to let go of whatever dream.

The Divine Spark

Remember, dear one, the nature of the Divine Spark. The Divine Spark is in you, it is in every other being and, although in some way dormant, in all that is.

It is your Divine Spark that has summoned you to embark on this journey back to you. It is your Divine Spark which always promised you that there was more to life than sleeping, eating, excreting and reproducing.

Now turn inside, and you will feel it again. It is always there. It has always been with you. Sometimes you will experience it as a bright, soft light; sometimes as an overwhelming feeling of love, sometimes as your own voice, sometimes as all of that simultaneously.

Remember that it is *mindfulness* that nourishes your Divine Spark.

It is mindfulness that makes you see things the way they really are—beyond the surface, beyond your current attachments, beyond the mass consciousness surrounding you right now.

Mindfulness is another notion of allowing to let go.

Being mindful means to be aware of what is going on inside yourself right *now*. Of the thoughts going through your mind, the emotions going through your body, the conditionings driving you at any given time.

Only by being in this state of mindfulness will you be able to give yourself permission to no longer follow that which is happening seemingly automatically inside of you.

Being mindful means to merge with the Divine Spark. The moment you do this, you cease to exist. Nothing of all that constitutes your personality can withstand mindfulness. What becomes of a conviction if you stop giving energy to it? What becomes of an aversion if you stop feeding it? What becomes of good and bad if you drop your concept of morals? What becomes of your past if you give yourself permission to forget yourself? What becomes of your future if you are able to drop all desires?

Remember: the more anchored you are in mindfulness, the clearer your Divine Spark will become. And the clearer your Divine Spark, the more profound mindfulness becomes. It is like a self-reinforcing process, a positive feedback loop that is eternally perpetuated.

It is the anchoring in your mindfulness, the embodiment of your Divine Spark that allows you to act in the world without obscuring your own Self through new kinds of attachments.

Remember that when you dissolve into the embodiment of the Divine Spark, nothing and nobody will be able to establish any relationship with you that is based on attachment. Attracted by your light, those around you will keep trying and trying and trying. But they will fail to find anything about you which they can hold on to. Your Divine Spark, the light of your consciousness, will become like a column of fire. Whatever is held into this fire, will also turn into fire, into awareness, into mindfulness, into the Divine Spark.

Remember that this divine type of existence is true compassion and therefore the source of *unconditional* love. By making your own light shine fully, you will create an atmosphere of total *acceptance*—acceptance of yourself, your environment and your fellow human beings. In this total acceptance, all judgment will disappear, which will allow everyone to be the way they happen to be at any given moment while they are in your presence. By fully accepting the other person, you will make them understand the good tidings that there is nothing they lack, that they are just as complete as you are.

Remember that you are not the only one walking this path. Instead, every single being is on it, and many have gone before you. Remember that to the degree that you are able to accept yourself ever more fully in all aspects and dimensions of your being, you will find it easier and easier to perceive the Divine Spark in everything. So you will rediscover yourself existing in a world full of awakened masters who have always supported you on your journey. Together with these awakened masters, you will play along the way.

It is this Divine Spark you share with all that is. It is this Divine Spark that is the one source of unity.

Suchness

Remember, dear one, the unlimited existence called *suchness*. By accepting everything the way it is, without seeing it through the lens of your own experience or expectations, you will enter the magical kingdom of suchness. In this kingdom, nothing will happen twice—everything is forever new. Every breath you take is *the one* breath. Every step you take is *the one* step. All of existence has moved towards this *one* moment. You are there in order to express and to celebrate it, solemnly, filled with awe, filled with the joy of being.

Remember that in the kingdom of suchness, nothing was ever born and nothing ever died. This kingdom of not holding on to things lies beyond time and, with this, beyond impermanence.

Walking in suchness is the path of the masters.

Suchness does not follow any particular purpose. Suchness means being for the sake of being. Through the lens of seeing differences, through the lens of duality, suchness cannot be discovered. Duality exists in the oscillation between pairs of opposites, in the swaying back and forth between small and large, bright and dark, right and wrong, good and bad, life and death. As soon as you cling on to even the smallest difference, you will drop out of the paradise of suchness into perishable existence right away.

Remember that the doorway to suchness is ever present. It is the gateless gate. Remember that this gate will be locked in the future. Remember that this gate was never opened in the past. This gate is something you can only walk through in the eternal *now*. The future will never create the conditions that will allow you to pass through this gate. Therefore do not wait until tomorrow or until circumstances will be more favorable.

Now—feel *this one outbreath*. No discrimination, no clinging on to things can withstand this single outbreath. Now—feel *this one inbreath*. Feel how, with this one inbreath, everything is being created anew, without the burden of the past, without the burden of any intent.

Now, my dear one, welcome your kingdom, the unlimited existence called suchness.

Creation

Remember, dear one, the spiritual physics which every creation in your sphere of existence is based upon. Both the formation of mental forms and their manifestation in the world of matter follow simple laws. You have been endowed with the ability to fully apply these laws.

Remember that *consciousness* and *emotions* are the keys to creation. Remember that to the degree to which you let go of your self-chosen limitations, the clarity of your consciousness and the intensity of your emotions will become stronger.

Remember that parts of our power of creation were known and practiced at all times. Prayer or conjuration, visualization or daydreams activate parts of the creative process.

There was a reason for you and the human race veiling your creative powers back then. Now the time has come to lift that veil again, so that the creator who you are can express itself through you in all its matured wisdom.

Before we can continue from here, remember once again the insufficiency of words and terminology. Do not absorb the following through your intellect, but sense the constant process of creation inside yourself and through yourself. Give your rational mind a break and give yourself permission to regain insight into the mystery of being.

Now look inside. Remember a moment of your life when you perceived an *intuition* in your consciousness. For an intuition to appear in your consciousness, it must cover a long distance and pass through many transformational processes. It comes to you as a creative impulse, as an *idea of expression*, either flowing out of your own creative source or by you responding to an already existing impulse.

Now sense how such an impulse initially needs to pass all your subconscious convictions and beliefs. Depending on how *limiting* your convictions and beliefs are, the original impulse will be *distorted*. Remember that it is your subconscious convictions in particular which *structure* the nature of reality. In fact, it is convictions, both your personal ones as well as the collective ones, which lead to the creation and maintenance of *any* type of structure.

Consciousness the way it is understood here is that which provides structure. Once again: *Consciousness the way it is understood here is that which provides structure.* As such, it is consciousness which structures both internal and external impressions according to its convictions at any given time and interprets them within the framework of its structuring. Be aware that the term *consciousness* here also includes what is frequently called the subconscious or unconscious. You yourself, however, are beyond consciousness. You are the *witness* of everything that is happening.

Now, remember that in the spiritual physics of creation, it does not matter whether you feed an impulse with the respective emotion consciously or unconsciously. The same applies to the required structure-forming consciousness. The efficiency of the processes of consciousness as it is understood here does not depend on the degree of your insight into the latter at any given moment.

Creative impulses will be reshaped by your own consciousness and therefore become thoughts. Remember that every thought has a *form*, which is also why we want to call it *thought form*. Every thought form has a particular degree of *vitality* that it owes to the *emotion* which becomes linked to the thought form. You could also say that the emotion gets *projected into* the thought form and virtually begins to soak it fully. The stronger the projected emotion, the more vital the thought form will be.

In all of existence, there are no two things that are identical. Just like there are no two identical grains of sand, there are no two identical thought forms. Every thought form has its own unique *energy signature*. Some people are able to perceive it physically and might translate it into something like a vibration, a sound, a color cloud, a complex geometrical structure, a specific emotion, or a light apparition.

A thought form is alive in the sense that it develops or changes depending on the consciousness energy or emotion it is being fed. The clearer, the stronger and the more constantly this thought form is being nourished by the consciousness energy and emotion, the stronger, the clearer and the more constant, and therefore the more vital, the respective energy signature becomes.

Like a magnet, thought forms have an impact on their realm of existence. However, since in the realm of thought forms something such as *space* does not exist, there is also no limitation to this impact. The *entire* realm of existence will immediately be *touched* by the energy signature of the thought form.

Therefore, every thought form is accessible for the witness, for *any* witness. Any witness, knowingly or unknowingly, can get in contact with any thought form via the *resonance principle*. Resonance enables every witness to pick up the creative impulse on which a thought form is based. A witness can accept it and begin to reinforce and develop the respective thought form by feeding it awareness and energy. On the other hand, witnesses can also reject it and then try to deny or ignore its existence or to even counter it via an opposed thought form. Moreover, witnesses are free to just stay neutral.

Also remember that, depending on how vital they are, thought forms also have the capacity to attract and structure the ubiquitous *latent energy* according to the resonance principle. It is this latent energy, which, driven by the vitality of the thought form, will manifest physically as matter.

Right here you will begin to get a glimpse of the fact that thought forms can take on any degree of complexity in the way they are arranged. Arrangements which are far beyond what you can possibly envision. Thought form arrangements can give rise to highly complex physical structures: elementary particles, atoms, molecules, molecule strands and structures, seemingly sentient and insentient objects of all kinds, all sizes and degrees of permanence.

For a moment, just feel the ramifications of what you have described to yourself so far. This universal principle creates individual form and structure, as well as collective form and structure. Philosophies, religions, world views, morals, races, species, instincts, conditionings, desires, intentions, telepathy, recollections of past lives and epochs, prophecies, even laws of nature—all these are reactions to originally creative impulses, cultivated and nourished by consciousness and emotion. My dear, are you beginning to regain a sense of how significant even the most inconspicuous thought must be?

Now, my dear creator, feel how everything *you believe to be* is ultimately a resonance with thought forms. Some of them you brought forth on your own, some of them you adopted. Being a witness, however, you have been endowed with the ability to either *initiate or stop any kind of resonance at will.* Furthermore, you have been equipped with the ability to materialize thought forms. Only because you do not always take the liberty to do so, you often need to take the long road in order to finally manifest a thought, an idea. Remember that materialization can follow different routes—for example, a clear idea, provided with a strong emotion, can be picked up and acted out by another person telepathically without this person being aware of it.

Remember that doubt and fear are also among the emotions you can project into your thought forms—either knowingly or unknowingly. Rest assured that, through resonance, the thought forms charged with these emotions will also attract corresponding energies and events and finally begin to manifest in your life.

Now, dear one, you got the keys back. *Use them well.*

You ask me what will happen if you stop resonating in the first place? You will find yourself back at the point before creation——and although I am using the word 'you' here, it won't be you.

Creation *in its fullness* happens in every single moment. Between two moments, however, there is timeless eternity.

Remember, dear one: In the timeless eternity between two moments, you will find an infinite number of doors to an infinite number of resonance systems. This is where all of creation originates, this is where you originate—this is the point in which creation flows back into the creator. Look into the eyes of a marveling child, and you will look directly into the source, directly into the heart of creation.

Authenticity

Remember, dear one, the uniqueness of your being. Never before did any being choose the path that you have chosen. Never before did any being explore existence the way you did. Never before did any being create the world for itself the way you created it. Never before did any being come to the point where you are standing right now. All beings create their own path, their own reality, their own *now*. By fully living from your own, innermost, alive truth, you acknowledge your own sovereignty. In such a moment, you are *authentic*.

Authenticity is not rooted in the urge to distinguish yourself from others. It does not stem from the desire to become an unmistakable individual, to stand out against the masses, or to attract attention. Authenticity does not require you to be on stage, it is not in need of applause, and does not need approval or rejection. Actual authenticity is self-sufficient—it is the solemn knowledge that you are expressing this very moment in harmony with the uniqueness of your being.

Remember that authenticity is nothing static. To the degree that you manage to penetrate into more profound insights and realization, your authenticity will take different forms of expression.

Authenticity is the inner compass that is always available to you, your signpost always showing you the right direction. Whatever step you take next—if it is rooted in your own authenticity, *it will be the right one*. May those around you say whatever they want: every such step, along with the experiences linked with it, will enrich you. It will expand both the spectrum of your authenticity and your reality.

Remember that the voice of your authenticity is very subtle. It might easily get superimposed by the voices of fear, of habit, of your upbringing, your culture and the mass. But if you listen closely to what is going on inside yourself, fully trusting that this voice exists, that your signpost cannot be separated from you, it will make itself known. Just be patient and wait. The moment you perceive this voice of your own authenticity, you will recognize it and have a sense of trueness. Later, doubts might surface, but know that these are only the whisperings of your fear. Do not fear, dear one.

Experiencing your own authenticity will allow you to accept all other beings along with exactly the choices they have made right *now*.

Authenticity culminates in experiencing and acknowledging your unique, unlimited being in the midst of limitless existence.

Focus

Remember, dear one, that at any time it is you yourself determining which dimensions of existence appear before the inner eye of your awareness. Just like you perceive the physical world through your physical senses, you perceive the infinite variety of the non-physical world via corresponding non-physical organs. Also remember that only a fraction of what you perceive actually manages to find the way to your inner eye. It is your *focus* that determines which particular impressions are actualized and, in doing so, it is your focus that will shape your reality from moment to moment.

By selecting a particular inner focus, you provide yourself with the opportunity for an utterly intense gathering of *experiences* within a restricted reality. While you are moving around in a reality that has been filtered this way, all events within this reality are reinforced like through a tremendously powerful magnifying glass. And this focus will allow you to *experience* this extract of reality *from the inside out* and to finally *master* it. To master means to become able to move freely and intimately *into* this extract of reality *and out of it* by *giving up your identification* with whatever gets realized in the extract of reality you selected.

By turning your focus inside and acknowledging that you actualize simultaneously a physical life in space, time and matter as well as a *non-physical existence* beyond space, time and matter, letting go of your identification with your body and your physical past will become easier and easier. Then, when the time has come, you will be able to experience your physical life as *an expression* of your non-physical existence. This is the moment when the mother of all fears—the fear of death—will have served its task and will welcome you in the midst of unlimited existence once again.

You know that, as a physical being, you are highly fixated on visual impressions. You expect physical phenomena to manifest as *images* in your consciousness. But remember, if you direct your focus inside, your primary sense organ for internal perception will be *sensation*. So you will need to develop great trust in your ability to sense things. Again and again, you will be seized by doubt, since you cannot see the inside world. Do not doubt, dear one. Know instead that whatever inner visions are created—as beautiful as they may be—these are *being projected by you yourself*. Therefore do not indulge in these visions. Instead, allow them perfect freedom. Allow them to change. Give them permission to disengage from whatever limitations continue to exist inside yourself. Grant them full freedom, so they can dissolve into the unlimited any time—only then can they help you to orient in this new world without getting caught in it.

Remember that the moment you place your focus on the inner world, your non-physical existence, both your body as well as the space around yourself will change. You will allow both of them to *relax*, to simply be—without any expectations, without any projections, without any rigid fixation by an omnipotent consciousness. Rooted in your non-physical existence, you can simply allow your body to be a body. Immediately, you will sense how the space inside and around your body assumes a neutral, peaceful state filled with potential. As soon as you then expand your focus to include this space around yourself, you will deliberately live simultaneously in your physical *and* non-physical realities. The energy field generated in such moments, with its particular alignment, will have an immediate impact on other human beings who happen to get in touch with it. It will enable them to spontaneously become aligned with this vibration of wholeness and limitlessness, this intuitive knowledge of their own home and this way to sense their own unlimited being. Remember that you, being beyond space, can manifest this energy field anywhere.

Realize that your existence is truly *multidimensional*. To the degree to which you allow the letting go to happen, and are able to dissolve attachments and limitations, you will be able to *rediscover, re-experience* and *relive* ever new dimensions and—ultimately master them.

It was your chosen focus propelling you through the lifetimes and ages, forgetting about your wholeness one time after the other, in order to, enhanced by authentic experience, open new ways for existence. It is now time for you to claim your full mastership in directing your focus. Remember, dear one: focus is the *Great Vehicle* between the dimensions.

Going Beyond

Remember, dear one, the limitlessness of existence and with it the limitlessness of knowledge, of wisdom and of the unknowable.

It is not that the prime of consciousness is somewhere in the past, in some eras of earlier times, in cultures which have long disappeared or in the hearts of masters who have gone out long ago. Existence as such has not placed any limitations upon itself. It is neither petty nor filled with anxiety—it is *creative*. So creative that it has not even *repeated itself once*, so limitless that it allows every wisdom to develop and to deepen, so overflowing that it is constantly in full bloom.

Therefore do not allow the teachings and views of the ancients to be the summit for you. After all, as beautiful as the view from the summit might be, from there, your path will only go downhill. Instead, allow them to be like the rungs of a ladder, a ladder which keeps growing and which is just as limitless as existence itself.

Remember that this, more than everything else, also applies to all the knowledge and wisdom you have seen for yourself. In the moment of seeing it: *Aaaah!* And then—let it go, *right away*. Limitless existence does not stand still, dear one. Do not take any luggage from the past with you. Yes, knowledge and wisdom can be used by you as medicine—for yourself, and perhaps for others. Just a little help, a little crutch meant to serve you for a brief period of time. And then—*leave it behind.*

The miracle of existence *cannot be known.* No thought can grasp it, no word can express it, no concept can explain it. Going beyond means diving into the unknowable again and again, to feel *unlimited existence* again and again. By immersing yourself into this ocean of unlimited existence again and again, it is as if you created waves. These waves travel far and allow the unlimited to go beyond itself.

Remember and know that you yourself are not knowable. And then, go beyond that—again and again and again . . .

Master

Remember, dear one, what it means to be a master. A master is not characterized by exceptional abilities, by an exceptional amount of knowledge or an exceptional amount of creativity. Although these features may be generated as a natural expression of the inner masterhood, they are neither required nor important. Instead, remember the one basic feature of a master: *A master allows every energy to serve him.*

Sense the meaning of this simple phrase, sense it profoundly. Remember that *serving* in the sense of supporting, giving, enlivening counts among the most fulfilling experiences. The service we are talking about here is not the kind of service based on dependency or fear. Therefore remember and get a sense that *every energy wants to serve*. Every energy wants to find its highest expression, wants to play with other energies.

For an energy to be able to serve you, only one thing is necessary: *accept it*. Accept it without any fear, say *Yes* to it. Absolutely assume that you are making a substantial contribution to a particular energy encountering you. You have never become a *victim* of any energy or *unworthy* of receiving an energy. By accepting an energy, by allowing it to *serve* you, it can become through you a higher expression of itself.

Remember that *only* by you *fully* accepting an energy, you will be in a position to *fully* deal with it. Only by accepting that you are the creator of an energy, will you enable yourself to handle it sovereignly. To the degree you do not accept an energy fully, it will seemingly begin to handle *you*— this way confirming you in your role as a victim or as an unworthy receiver. Be aware that in these cases, too, the energy served you in reconfirming your choice.

Now go inside and feel what it means to say *Yes* to all energies surrounding you right now. It is not necessary for you to *understand* why you created this or that—there are internal reasons for this in you which by far go beyond any limited rational understanding. Instead, simply say *Yes*. Feel that in such a moment you are in the midst of a friendly universe, surrounded by energies you accept and which are waiting to serve you. Acting from this knowledge, expressing yourself, and therefore going beyond yourself by accepting all that is, means *masterhood*.

Masterhood exists only in the *now*.

Remember that masterhood is not a title that will be granted to you by any external source. Do not allow yourself to be misled by such things. In the now of your masterhood, you will not need any acknowledgement, and this is exactly how the entire cosmos will acknowledge you.

Now, my dear master, simply say *Yes*. That's how simple things are.

Purpose

Remember, dear one, the tie of the *purpose of life*. Purpose is one of the subtlest ties preventing you from awakening to your wholeness. First of all, relearn to see that whatever purpose there might be, it does not come from you: It might have arisen from your upbringing, from your religion or some kind of longing, some kind of curiosity, some kind of despair—anyway, it always came from *external sources*, it always required *the other*. In your culture or in the age you live in, it might be appreciated, or it might be dreaded or looked down upon—you have chosen this purpose based on encouragement by *others*.

Almost everybody will agree with you saying how important it is to find the purpose of your life and to act accordingly—to act in a way that *follows a particular purpose*, to allow this *purpose to guide your actions*. This type of actions will again have an impact on you and will in turn reinforce the importance of your currently adopted purpose.

See that every purposeful action will establish a relationship meant to serve whatever purpose you have in mind. The more important you take yourself and your life's purpose, the more effort you will make to act purposefully, which will virtually result in a huge network of purpose-oriented relationships.

Depending on how skillfully you go about this, this network will fulfill its purpose—and end up confirming how valuable your chosen purpose is, how valuable *you* are, which might cause you to *stay stuck* in feeling acknowledged. Or else, your network simply becomes complicated, unsightly and does not fulfill the functions it was supposed to fulfill—and so you will feel miserable, not knowing why you exist in the first place.

Be happy, dear one, be happy if you fail to achieve your purpose! Although—if you were to achieve it—there might come a moment when you find yourself saying, "Enough!". You are tired of tasting this purpose and might turn your back on it. However, you, having become addicted to success and acknowledgement, will most likely be drawn to turning to a new purpose, a new network, a new kind of enmeshment. Failure, on the other hand, makes it easier for you to see through the senselessness of any kind of purpose.

Now begin to feel that you are a *wholeness*, feel that you are complete. There is nothing you lack. There is nothing which needs to be granted to you from any *external* source. Go inside and feel what it means if, out of ignorance, a wholeness imposes a purpose on itself, trying to act according to this purpose in an effort to become whole again. Every purpose *will always obscure your wholeness*. Caught in the attempt to find a way back to your own wholeness by becoming the expression of a purpose, you will actually keep splitting off more and more of this wholeness of yours. In your purpose-driven actions, you will sense deep inside that you are constantly getting further and further away from yourself, no matter how much applause or other kind of confirmation you might be receiving from the external world.

You are wondering how to get out of these tricky involvements?

Remember, dear one: *there is no path to your own wholeness!*

After all, every path would only end up being yet another purpose, yet another set of actions, yet another network. Perhaps you will then call it spiritual. Perhaps it will make those around you cherish you even more—but you will only find yourself in another trap.

Instead, consider the idea that your existence does not require any sense of purpose. Feel deep inside what it means to be whole. So whole that you are able to face every being, every event, every situation without seeing any purpose in it. There is nothing you need to be granted by others, since you are already whole. It is not about establishing a relationship which would be limited by any particular purpose. There is nothing but wholeness expressing itself completely. Completely in the sense that no expectations with regard to any future results are involved. The expression *as such* is complete, fully and totally perfected, *free from any expectations* with regard to the future.

Remember, letting go of any kind of purpose implies nothing but the fact that your actions become profoundly free from your personal desire to achieve wholeness. This letting go will allow your actions to come from a totally new level. Free from the need to serve you, they will be able to unfold in their own way. See that they will be blessed by your own wholeness, that they will bear the taste of wholeness and therefore inspire everything and everybody to acknowledge and unfold their own wholeness.

It is in allowing your wholeness that you will make your existence transcend any kind of purpose. It is in acting from a place free from any kind of purpose, simply as an expression of your wholeness, that you will be able to touch all of existence profoundly and to allow it to unfold in ever increasing wholeness.

The One Breath

Remember, dear one, the incomparable magic of the *One Breath*. No teacher, no master, no ritual, no initiation and no religion has even remotely the transforming power of the *One Breath*.

The One Breath does not have any prerequisites. It does not depend on whether you happen to be a man or a woman in this lifetime, whether you are already old or still young, or on how intelligent or knowing or wise you are. The One Breath is possible anytime—and it will immediately give your life a new direction.

Remember that the human mind, the human ego, is constantly looking for ways to delay its own awakening. After all, in awakening this ego would loose its all-determining role. It would no longer be the author and the main character in the drama of its own life. It would be challenged to jump head-on into the unknown, it would be challenged to allow *change* to happen, it would be challenged to give up *control*. As a result, this anxious human ego resorts to a simple trick: It pretends to fulfill your deepest longing for wholeness by committing itself to something which in one way or the other *requires time*. It says: "Awakening is possible—*later!*" And so it will remain in its illegitimate position as a limited master in an unlimited house.

Try to grasp the truth of what has just been said deep inside. *Feel the fear of your ego towards letting your own story go!*

Understand that the paths you have walked so far are paths that ultimately prevented you from *totally* allowing the letting go to happen. They might have supported you for a while, they might have rewarded you with comfort and company. Honor yourself and the efforts you have made so far. Honor yourself for them—and see that your step towards wholeness requires you to go beyond all that.

Only continue reading, dear one, if you can follow these explanations in your heart and if you agree with them. Only then! If not, if you are still convinced that the awakening will only take place later or that it will require the intervention of somebody else or of some higher power, then *continue to follow the path you are on right now.* Wait until your inner voice clearly tells you, "Now!".

***

Now that you have become one with me, *your* notes, come very close and feel the essence of all your efforts of your lifetimes. Now is the moment when you can once again take the only step that matters. Everything beautiful, everything good will automatically follow. Now relax, feel your entire body, be fully and totally *in* your body. And in this being present, *breathe in.* There is *just this inbreath*— nothing else. Then, in this being present, *breathe out.* There is *just this outbreath*—nothing else. This is the key. There is nothing that could be simpler. There is nothing that could be more profound.

With this *one inbreath* you are saying *Yes* to life, you are saying *Yes* to your body, to every cell, to your entire being. This full inbreath is the only elixir of life—it is life itself.

With this one *outbreath*, you let go of the past. The remote past, the recent past. Nothing can withstand this one outbreath, no thought, no theory, no story, no desire. You become totally free, ready to receive and to express life anew.

The One Breath does not have any before or after. It is pure presence, transcending all of time. And in the One Breath, there is also no room for an anxious ego trying to hold on. See that this One Breath does not require any *process*, any evolution. You simply let it happen.

Just like the very first thing a child does after having been born is breathe in, and just like the very last thing a dying person does before her death, is breathe out, this One Breath is a complete cycle in itself. In this One Breath you will be able to transcend yourself, to go beyond life and death, right into your own wholeness.

See, dear one, you needed to go through all these efforts, through all your searching in the external world, through all your begging from others, you needed to fail in all your endeavors in order to ultimately find yourself having been left to your own devices.

It is only in this moment that you will be able to discover and acknowledge your own treasure.

Everybody carries this treasure of his or her own wholeness inside. From now on, you will be able to see this treasure in everyone, you will be able to sense your similarities, your kinship and your connectedness with every single being.

Others will approach you asking questions. But you know that words do not really help. Instead, breathe the One Breath. Invite the other person to simply breathe with you. Remember, the One Breath is the greatest gift you can ever give to yourself and others.

Everyday Life

Remember, dear one, that an awakened life is being actualized *in every single moment*. Such a moment *does not require any particular context*. It is only in this very moment, just the way it is, that an enlightened life becomes possible. Do not wait for conditions to be better—they will never arrive. By fully entering into this moment, you will go beyond all conditions.

The true temple resides in you—it is unparalleled by any external temple. Even if you feel the desire to regularly withdraw into this *Inner Temple*, remember that it is your everyday life providing your Inner Temple with its glamour. By receiving your everyday life while being rooted in your own Inner Temple, you will be able to touch everything in its depth. You can look through the seeming reality of all outer appearance directly into the heart of every phenomenon and by this means enlighten yourself.

Remember that the circumstances of your everyday life will continue evolving along with your own evolution. Enter your Inner Temple again and again and watch the miracle of change from there. Allow that which you call everyday life to be a constant invitation to fill your Inner Temple with life.

What is good? What is bad? What is profane? What is sacred? From your Inner Temple, you will not look through the lens of differences, but see with the *eye of preciousness*. Knowing about your own unconditional preciousness, which is becoming actualized in this very moment, you will recognize the same preciousness in all.

Your everyday life will be the playing field which again and again will provide you with very personal opportunities for an ever more profound letting go, for an ever more profound acceptance, for an ever more profound understanding, for an ever more profound existence.

Remember that the moment when you completely accept existence *just the way it is* equals the moment of complete letting go. In this very moment, your Inner Temple will be completely unlimited. Everyday life? Temple? Everyday life *is* the temple. The temple *is* everyday life.

The Final Birth

Remember, dear one, the grace of death. It is physical death that enables your being to let go of many frozen attachments. Without physical death, the wheel of your attachments would keep turning and turning. By means of death it becomes easier for you to gain more profound insights into existence.

However, you should also remember that your existence without a physical body is not really different from your existence in a physical body. Profound attachments remain even after death, searching for a new expression. Therefore do not seek death, since this rejection of life would then persist as such a profound attachment in your being. Instead, see life and death like seasons, one replacing the other. Summer and winter each have their own beauty.

If you give yourself permission to remember even more profoundly, you will once again become aware that there is a kind of birth requiring neither an external mother nor an external father. This will be your final birth—if you so choose. For this birth, you are *your own mother and your own father;* you are the mother energy and the father energy. Both energies are contained in your being from the very beginning. In fact, it is the separation between these two that is continued in the discriminating mind.

If you are ready, you can allow both of these energies to reunite in you. This unification will bring forth something new, *a new energy,* which you can neither conceive of nor intuit.

Remember that this unification is not about somehow embellishing or magnifying your life, the circumstances of your life, or your personal story. You will allow for your story to simply drop away from you, *just the way it happens to be at that very moment.* You will leave your story behind just like you left your dead body behind so many times.

Are you ready for this?

Notice that this does not imply running away or escaping. Do not think in terms of responsibility or obligation—by letting go of your personal story, you will be able to encounter those around you in a totally new way. Allowing yourself to blossom is the greatest gift you can give to existence. *All of existence* is longing for you to give this wonder to yourself.

See that during your journey through all these lifetimes, you have always been searching for that part of the female or male energy that happened to express itself less in you at any given moment. You were always on the lookout for this missing piece of the puzzle in the external world. No matter how beautiful a moment was, you were always aware that there was something which had not yet been completed totally, that there was something which somehow was not in balance yet.

If you are ready again, if you would like to allow your true birth to happen, then go inside. Feel your female energy, feel your male energy and allow the two of them to meet. In the initial moment of them touching, you will simultaneously experience a love and sexual arousal you have never known before.

Allow both of them to surface, dear one, allow both of them to surface. It took so long to make this encounter possible, so long. From this point on, surrender totally to this new love. It is new because it cannot be compared to anything you used to call love before. Surrender to this new love for yourself which you can feel inside. Don't do anything, just allow. Your personal story, the way you used to live it so far, will become like a flower of emptiness. As for you, this new energy will provide you with a kind of fulfillment that goes beyond everything you ever imagined.

Perhaps, dear one, just perhaps, you already realized this final birth of yours at an earlier time. Perhaps you allowed the veil of forgetfulness to descend over you once again in order to re-embark on the journey through life. Now that you have experienced the derangement being brought about by a lifetime of separation as well as the allowing of this new energy once again, you can truly be helpful for others. But do not proselytize and do not have any expectations. Just make yourself available. Allow existence to take care of itself by letting it make just the right encounters happen at just the right time.

Epilogue

Now, dear one, it is about time for us to go beyond our journey. Do not hold on to me, your records. Once again, honor yourself for your path, since it was perfect. Give me, as an expression of yourself, permission to enjoy complete freedom and unfolding.

We will meet again when the time is ripe—in a new form, in a new disguise—and share the adventures of our existence with each other.

*

Made in the USA
Las Vegas, NV
23 March 2022